T Shirt Printing and Promotional Clothing Buyers Guide
Money Saving Tips for Marketing and Company Apparel

Heidi Thorne

Copyright © 2012, 2014
All rights reserved.

ISBN-13: 978-1480296282
ISBN-10: 1480296287

All rights reserved. No part of this publication may be reproduced, stored in a retrieval system, or transmitted in any form or by any means, electronic, mechanical, recording or otherwise, without the prior written permission of the author.

Limit of Liability/Disclaimer of Warranty: Both the publisher and author have used their best efforts in preparation of this book. No representations or warranties for its contents, either expressed or implied, are offered or allowed and both parties disclaim any implied warranties of merchantability or fitness for your particular purpose. The advice and strategies presented herein may not be suitable for you, your situation or business. Consult with a professional advisor where and when appropriate. Neither the publisher nor author shall be liable for any loss of profit or any other commercial damages, including but not limited to special, incidental, consequential, or other damages.

First Edition, 2012. Updated November 2014, January 2016.

Thorne Communications LLC
www.ThorneCommunications.com

T Shirt Printing and Promotional Clothing Buyers Guide
Money Saving Tips for Marketing and Company Apparel

Heidi Thorne

TABLE OF CONTENTS

NO SUCH THING AS A CHEAP T SHIRT vii

CHAPTER 1: PROMOTIONAL T SHIRTS: WHY NOT TO BUY THEM 1

CHAPTER 2: UNDERSTANDING THE BUYING PROCESS FOR NEWBIES 3

CHAPTER 3: 7 THINGS YOU NEED TO KNOW WHEN ORDERING IMPRINTED T SHIRTS 6

CHAPTER 4: WHAT DOES T SHIRT WEIGHT OZ. MEAN AND WHY IS IT IMPORTANT? 9

CHAPTER 5: CURE FOR THE COMMON T SHIRT 11

CHAPTER 6: SET UP CHARGES FOR T SHIRT SCREEN PRINTING EXPLAINED AND 4 WAYS TO REDUCE YOUR COST 12

CHAPTER 7: 5 TIPS TO GET YOUR CUSTOM T SHIRT AND PROMOTIONAL CLOTHING ORDERS ON TIME 15

CHAPTER 8: 4 TIPS FOR HANDLING RUSH T SHIRT ORDERS 20

CHAPTER 9: WHAT IS "GOOD ARTWORK" FOR IMPRINTING? 22

CHAPTER 10: 6 GUIDELINES GRAPHIC DESIGNERS NEED TO KNOW WHEN DESIGNING FOR T SHIRTS 25

CHAPTER 11: HOW TO IMPRINT QR CODES ON T SHIRTS .. 28

CHAPTER 12: 10 THINGS YOU NEED TO KNOW WHEN ORDERING EMBROIDERED APPAREL 31

CHAPTER 13: STITCH COUNT FOR CUSTOM EMBROIDERY EXPLAINED 35

CHAPTER 14: DEBOSSED LEATHER IMPRINTING EXPLAINED 38

CHAPTER 15: HOW TO AVOID A PUBLIC RELATIONS NIGHTMARE WHEN BUYING PROMOTIONAL CLOTHING .. 40

CHAPTER 16: WHAT DOES MADE IN THE USA REALLY MEAN? 43

CHAPTER 17: WHAT IS A UNION BUG? 45

CHAPTER 18: IS YOUR PROMOTIONAL T SHIRT MADE OF UNNATURAL COTTON? 47

CHAPTER 19: HOW TO GREEN UP PROMOTIONAL T SHIRT BUYING WITH LIFE CYCLE ASSESSMENT 50

CHAPTER 20: HOW TO START AN ECO FRIENDLY CASUAL FRIDAY 54

CHAPTER 21: SHOULD YOU SELL YOUR BRANDED T SHIRTS? 57

CHAPTER 22: THINKING BEYOND THE T SHIRT 60

ABOUT HEIDI THORNE 61

NO SUCH THING AS A CHEAP T SHIRT

Year after year, one promotional product category takes top spot on the Advertising Specialty Institute State of the Industry report: shirts. In fact, in the 2012 rankings, it captured 20 percent of the year's total reported revenues for the entire industry. That is huge! And it's a good indicator of their enduring popularity to promote businesses and causes.

What isn't reported are the actual number of shirts and the percentage of screen printed T shirts versus embroidered shirts. But from my experience, I will tell you that shirts, on a per piece basis, are an expensive promotional investment that must be chosen with care.

Adding to the expense factor is the ROI (return on investment) issue. Buying shirts with logos is a public relations and branding expense that may not lead directly to a sale. But where shirts do earn their keep is by increasing the number of impressions that your logo and company name receive when they are worn AND seen by your target audience. A promotional T shirt worn as a pajama top gets little exposure. So, again, carefully choosing appropriate wearable items for your purpose and people is critical to making this a worthwhile use of your marketing and promotion dollars.

Plus there is a myriad of details that, if you're not paying attention, can drive up the cost of a promotional shirt project in a flash. Set up charges, artwork fees, shipping… it all adds up.

So my intent in writing this book is to help T shirt and promotional clothing buyers, like you, understand the process so that you can save money while saving your organization's image.

Heidi Thorne

CHAPTER 1: PROMOTIONAL T SHIRTS: WHY NOT TO BUY THEM

What? A promotional product marketing consultant is telling me NOT to buy T shirts? Shocking!

In addition to possibly being an expensive and sometimes ineffective promotion, buying T shirts that may have limited use can also be a very un-green thing to do at your event or tradeshow. Here's why...

First of all, you have the sizing issues. Unless you know the sizes of your recipients in advance, you are going to be spending a lot of money to buy a lot of different sizes to accommodate everyone. Otherwise, everybody is going to have to wear these big, baggy XXL T shirts. I really think that is just a waste of money, because at the end of the event, you are going to have a whole bunch left over of sizes that nobody wanted, and you are either going to have to recycle them or you are going to have to donate them to Goodwill or other charity.

The second reason I would not suggest them is that some people feel uncomfortable wearing them at the event. It depends on the event. If it is a running event, a walk or some other kind of casual family type of event, people often expect to receive T shirts. So certainly buy them for those kinds of events. But for corporate, unless you make it part of an activity at an event, don't buy them.

The other thing is that they are expensive. There is no such thing as a cheap T shirt. I don't know if people really realize that, but T shirts are expensive. There is not only the cost of the shirt, but the cost of decorating and set up, especially if you want your name on the front and back. So as your promotional products consultant and advisor, I am going to tell you to think twice before you just automatically go for a promotional T shirt.

CHAPTER 2:
UNDERSTANDING THE BUYING PROCESS FOR NEWBIES

We'd like you to order up some new company T shirts for us. You need to get up to speed on buying this type of thing... fast!

Here is some important real world knowledge about the T shirt buying process...

Prices and Products are Not the Same as at Target or Wal-Mart. Newer and less experienced buyers are usually sticker-shocked at how much an item will cost when purchased for promotional purposes. *But I can get a Hanes T shirt at Target for $3!* they muse when their consultant quotes a price of $6 for what they feel is the same shirt with just some printing on it. In some cases it might be the same shirt or something very similar.

Here's the situation. Large retailers are buying product by the truckloads. Notice that it is truckloads with a "s." They have huge centralized buying forces that negotiate based on volume and many other factors such as shipping. Your 144 piece order is a short, special order run even for the consultant and his suppliers. Plus, you are buying occasionally and they usually don't know when your next order might come in. Thus the higher pricing to cover their costs to handhold you through your order without guarantees for future business. Additionally, your consultant or decorator incurs costs to set up presses and process your order. These are also built into your price.

You Need "Good" Art. If you email a JPEG file of your logo to your promotional product consultant, first he'll just shake his head and say, *Not another one.* In this situation, your consultant may ask you to provide electronic artwork in a "vector" format such as Encapsulated Postscript (.eps) or Adobe Illustrator (.ai). These formats provide clean-edged art that is required for imprinting and can usually be provided by your company's graphic designer. If you cannot provide the proper artwork, you may charged an art clean-up fee to make it print-ready.

Your Consultant May Not be Printing Your T shirts in His Office. Promotional products, including T shirts, are typically imprinted at large facilities that can handle orders of hundreds or thousands pieces each. Your consultant may not be printing them for you at his or her company location. So suggesting that you can pick up your order at your consultant's office to save some time or shipping costs will not always be possible.

Shipping and Handling Costs and Issues Can be Huge. After the product price sticker shock, shipping and handling fees are often the aftershock. There are multiple issues.

First, a single tote bag or T shirt may seem like a small item. Now multiply that by 1,000 or more. The sheer physical volume of a large quantity of promotional products can overwhelm your office or dock. Also, thousands of boxed up pieces could be of significant weight, maybe even into the hundreds or thousands of pounds. Ask your consultant for information on the shipment size and weight and how it will be delivered to you so you can plan accordingly. While you're at it, ask them for an estimated shipping cost, too.

Second, expedited shipping is very, very, very expensive! In many cases, your product will not be shipping from the person or company from which are buying. It may be shipping across the country to your door. Many consultants do their best to look for the closest suppliers to shorten shipping time and cost. So allow for sufficient time to get the product produced plus the time to ship to you.

Now that you know more about the promotional products industry and the buying process, you won't be sending out a newbie alert when you contact your promotional consultant.

CHAPTER 3:
7 THINGS YOU NEED TO KNOW WHEN ORDERING IMPRINTED T SHIRTS

So you need to order some T shirts for an event. Well, that should be easy, right? Do you want to take a guess at how many choices you have? One of the imprinted apparel industry's leading warehousing suppliers has over 300 different T shirts in its inventory. 300! Then there are decorating options. Do you want the front or back or both decorated? Maybe the sleeves, too? How many colors should be printed? Overwhelming!

This is where a promotional products consultant can be your best friend. Based on your needs, he or she can help narrow the field and still stay within your budget. Let's dispel one myth right away. There is no such thing as a standard promotional T shirt. So let's look at what you need to consider when buying.

1. Fabric Content. 100 percent cotton or a 50/50 blend of cotton and a synthetic fiber are most common. Many people feel that all cotton T shirts are more comfortable. However, blended fabrics are often less wrinkly and are sometimes softer than all cotton. Time of year and preference of those who will be wearing the shirts will dictate.

2. *Fit.* Most men's T shirts are cut with a boxy shape, making them usable for both sexes. If you do not know how many women and men will be receiving your shirts, opt for the men's cut to cover all bases. Ladies fit shirts vary widely in cut and sizing and are best avoided for new buyers of promotional apparel. Children's sized shirts are also available. But you will have to have a pretty clear idea of the age and sizing you will need when ordering.

3. *Eco Friendly/Fair Trade Options.* For markets or groups that are sensitive to eco friendly issues, there are shirts made with organic cotton that do not use pesticides, herbicides, or genetically modified (GMO) seeds. As well, organic farming uses water management as opposed to heavy irrigation. Organic cottons must carry a certification of their organic farming, harvesting, and processing methods. Fair trade selections, some of them also being organic, prohibit the use of child, forced or prison labor in the manufacture of the materials or the assembly process.

4. *Colors.* White is the least expensive choice. Heathers, which are often used in athletic wear, are a middle priced option. Black and colors are most expensive. Your budget will dictate here.

5. *Imprinting.* Screen printing is the most common method for decorating promotional T shirts. One color imprinting is the least expensive since there are additional set up and running charges for multiple colors. If your logo is multi-colored, have your graphic designer reinterpret the design to black and white art (no gray allowed). Vector art, which is typically an Encapsulated Postscript (.eps) or Adobe Illustrator (.ai) file, is usually required for screen printing. Again, your graphic designer can assist in preparing your artwork.

6. *Imprint Locations.* Typically a full front, left chest, or full back imprint are the most commonly used locations for shirts. Occasionally, the edges of short sleeves or the full length of a long-sleeve shirt are used. However, be aware that as you add up the locations, your set up and running charges add up, too. Best to stick with maybe the front and/or back for cost savings. Your promotional products consultant can provide you with artwork sizes to pass along to your graphic designer.

7. *Quantities.* While promotional T shirts can be sold by the single piece or in dozen quantities, they are typically sold by the case size of 72 for best pricing. Some promotional product consultants or decorators will not accept orders less than 72. Quantities less than that may be cost prohibitive for you. Your consultant can help you determine what is possible for you.

CHAPTER 4:
WHAT DOES T SHIRT WEIGHT OZ. MEAN AND WHY IS IT IMPORTANT?

If you've ever shopped for promotional imprinted T shirts, you've likely encountered an ounce weight in a product description such as 5.5 oz., 6.1 oz. or 4.5 oz. Does that mean the shirt weighs that much or what?

Technically, the ounce weight means that a square yard of the T shirt fabric weighs that many ounces. So for a 6.1 oz. T shirt, a square yard of the fabric weighs 6.1 oz. As logic would dictate, the heavier the ounce weight, the thicker and heavier the T shirt.

Ounce weight of a T shirt is important to know so that you can select a shirt that's appropriate for your marketing purpose. Most standard T shirts are in the 4.5 oz. to 6 oz. range. Below that, the fabrics are light weight and may not be very durable which might be appropriate for some applications such as one-time event use. Additionally, some lightweight T shirts are tissue, sheer or fine jersey which are popular for some markets, such as for women's fashion wear. If you're looking for T shirts that will get heavy wear and tear, such as for uniform or construction use, generally a thicker weight of 6.0 oz. or above would be recommended.

Another reason ounce weight of a T shirt is important is because it will affect how much it is to ship from your consultant and/or decorator to you. The heavier the shirts, the heavier the boxes or the more boxes you may have to ship. T shirts are a heavy promotional item! A regular T shirt could weigh up to a half pound by itself depending on the fabric and design. Multiply that by hundreds... you get the idea. So unless you're doing a special type of T shirt, it's generally best to source as close to you as possible to avoid high freight costs which could run into the hundreds of dollars.

CHAPTER 5:
CURE FOR THE COMMON T SHIRT

Looking for a cool way to distribute a plain old T shirt? Then consider a compressed T shirt!

A compressed T shirt is a standard printed shirt that's subjected to hundreds of pounds of pressure to create a wide variety of shapes. Everything from cars, bottles, animals, tools, geometric shapes, product packages such as cans… you name it, there's probably a shape for it.

After being shaped, a colorful liner is packaged with the shirt and the whole thing is shrink wrapped. The liner offers you the opportunity to print your logo, graphics, coupons, QR codes and more to build your marketing brand.

These packages get a LOT of attention and are usually a "gotta get one" type of promotion. They can also be turned into direct mail pieces.

One of the issues that does come up with these shirts is that the wrinkles may not completely come out upon immediately opening. They usually relax after the first couple of washes.

To see examples, watch our compressed T shirt video on YouTube at http://youtu.be/2xNA6ULGNrA

CHAPTER 6:
SET UP CHARGES FOR T SHIRT SCREEN PRINTING EXPLAINED AND 4 WAYS TO REDUCE YOUR COST

Going to answer some comments that we got from one of our Promo With Purpose Today newsletter subscribers. I don't even know if I really want to call them comments. It was more of a frustration about set up charges.

First of all, let's explain what a set up charge is for T shirt printing. A set up charge is the cost to actually set up your order. It would typically include the cost to create and set up the screens for the printing machines. It could include maintenance on the machine. It could include the labor cost for their personnel to set up and run the machines. It could include ink charges. Just a lot of different things get rolled into it. And this is on top of the cost to create T shirt artwork design or to make your artwork print production ready.

If you see a product description that says there are no set up charges, it's not that there is no set up cost. It's just that those costs are rolled into the price of the printed T shirts in some other way.

The actual charges that get assessed depend on how complex your particular project is. A standard one-color imprint is relatively inexpensive. But if you imprint multiple colors or have other special handling—such such as a non-standard location for your imprint, special effect printing, flashing (a base coat of ink sometimes required when printing light colors on dark surfaces) or multiple locations—your cost could run into the hundreds of dollars.

Set up charges are not going to go away anytime soon. So you do need to budget for them when planning your T shirt screen printing project. Your promotional products consultant can help you determine what your set up costs will be.

Sure, some set up charges seem outrageous, especially on smaller quantity orders where the cost can add significantly to the per piece cost of your promotion. So how can you save money?

1. Order Larger Quantities. If you buy your promotional products in larger quantities for use over a longer period of time, those costs become less when spread out over the entire order.

2. Reuse Imprint Artwork. Depending on the supplier, sometimes they will let you use the same artwork on a reorder for no additional set up charge if your order is placed within a certain period of time, usually within three months to one year. Check with your consultant for details.

3. Simplify Your Artwork. The fewer the number of colors and the less complex your imprint design, the cheaper the set up charge.

4. Select Products with Standard Imprint Processes. Some imprint processes such as full color imprinting and embroidery have higher set up costs. Select products that use standard and less expensive processes such as ink imprinting.

CHAPTER 7:
5 TIPS TO GET YOUR CUSTOM T SHIRT AND PROMOTIONAL CLOTHING ORDERS ON TIME

Had an important concern about promotional products come in from one of our Promo With Purpose Today email subscribers: *Getting promotional products orders in timeframe promised.* That's a loaded issue! But we'll expose some secrets about promotional product and custom T shirt ordering so you can be in the know.

Production Time

When you look at various promotional item descriptions, you'll often see a "Production Time" estimate listed. What does this mean? That is the actual time it takes for a clothing decorator to apply your imprint to your shirts. This is NOT the entire time it takes to complete the order. Typically, the "production time" clock doesn't start ticking until the order and artwork are received and approved by the decorating company doing the imprinting for your promotional product consultant.

And usually, the production time begins the day AFTER the order is received by the decorator.

Many decorators also have daily cutoff times for receipt of orders. For example, let's say a decorator has established a 2:00 p.m. Central Time cutoff for receipt of orders to be placed into production the FOLLOWING business day. Let's also say that in this example your promotional consultant sends your order to the decorator at 3:00 p.m. Central Time on a Monday. That order will not go into production until Wednesday. So if there is a 3-day production time on this example order, it would not normally ship until late Friday.

On top of that, it may take your promotional consultant a day or two to check and prepare artwork and place the order. If you do not have "good artwork" (see the chapter on *What is Good Artwork for Imprinting?* for details), meaning it is not in a vector-based electronic file (a Encapsulated Postscript .eps or Adobe Illustrator .ai file are industry standard), it could take several additional days to prepare your imprint for production. Plus, your promotional product consultant may charge you to make your artwork production ready if it is not.

And I need to emphasize that production and order processing time are BUSINESS days, not including weekends or holidays.

Agreed, this is very confusing for customers. Unfortunately, published information fed to promotional shopping sites from manufacturers states only the in-house production time.

TIP #1: *Add at least 4 days to any published production time to complete your order if your* artwork is production-ready; more if it is not. And don't forget to add shipping time.

Production Exceptions

There are some special scenarios in regard to production time:

Rush Service. Many promotional consultants offer a rush promo service so you can get your promotional items fast. But there are caveats. First and foremost, you must be able to provide production-ready correctly-sized artwork for your consultant. If you do not have that, there will be additional time (and usually expense) required and rush service will not be available for your order. As well, watch for cutoff times. For example, we have a 9:00 a.m. Central Time cutoff. If not received by that time, it will be processed the following day. Shipping time needs to be added to this and will depend on the type of service you choose (ground, 2-day, overnight, etc.).

TIP #2: Watch for cutoff times on rush order service; add shipping time.

Peak Seasons. During peak seasons for T shirts, decorators are up to their eyeballs in orders, often doing double and weekend shifts to meet demand. They will attempt to meet published production times, but often physically cannot. Therefore, your production time could be extended by up to 5 to 7 working days during the peak seasons and express shipping may be required to meet any in-hand date you might have.

Peak seasons include: Start of School Year (August and September); Elections (usually spring and fall, especially during presidential election years); Sports (usually spring and fall sports are biggest); and, Special Events (again, usually spring and fall are busiest).

TIP #3: During peak seasons, particularly spring and fall, prepare for longer production times (add at least a week) and/or expedited shipping to meet your target dates.

Shipping Times

This is where it gets very confusing for customers. People often like to buy local and will place an order with a local promotional consultant. This may be a shock to many, but promotional product orders are rarely physically produced by the consultant you place the order with. Your consultant may be working with dozens or even hundreds of warehouses from coast to coast, or even overseas, depending on the item. Though some might, rarely do consultants or decorators have a huge inventory of blank stock on hand at their office or shop. So the product order you place with your local consultant in New York may actually be shipping from Florida… and then it has to go to the decorator to be imprinted. Luckily, many of the large T shirt and blank promotional apparel warehouses have locations throughout the country to reduce freight costs and shipping times. But if you have your heart set on a particular T shirt that's only available from a warehouse in California, expect to wait longer for your order to get done. Your promotional product consultant can advise choices that are available closer to home.

For ground shipping, it could take up to 5 business days (in the continental U.S.) after the order is produced to ship via ground to you after it is decorated. Add to that the time it takes to ship the blank product to the decorator.

TIP #4: *To allow for shipping within the United States, estimate at least 5 to 10 shipping days for domestic orders placed within the continental U.S. (more for Alaska or Hawaii).*

Doing the Math

Okay, let's walk through an example...

Time to process your order and artwork by your promotional product consultant and decorator: *2 to 4 business days, depending on condition of your artwork.*

Time to get blank T shirt stock: *1 to 5 business days.*

Time to imprint your T shirts: *5 to 7 business days.*

Time to ship/deliver your complete order: *1 to 5 business days, depending on your location.*

So to receive this item, you would need to place this order at least 11 to 20 business days prior to your target in-hand date, provided that your artwork is production-ready. That between 2 to 4 weeks!

With that, I'll leave you with the best tip of all...

TIP #5: *Plan ahead, it's later than you think.*

CHAPTER 8:
4 TIPS FOR HANDLING RUSH T SHIRT ORDERS

Okay, here's a confession. Sometimes I'm the promotional products consultant who doesn't get promo ordered early for my next event. It's the old plumber with the leaky faucet scenario again. However, I usually can rectify the situation in a short period of time, and not because I'm in the promo business either. It's because I use these rush order handling tips:

1. Develop a List of Go-To Suppliers for Rush Projects. I have two absolutely awesome suppliers who can turn orders around for me and ship them out the next business day or two if I get my order in by a designated time. Establish relationships with dependable go-to sources that you can rely on when the pressure's on. Develop those relationships BEFORE you need them. Familiarize yourself with their product offerings so you know what your options are.

2. Have Your Production-Ready Artwork Ready to Go at All Times. Clean, vector artwork is an absolute necessity for promotional product imprinting. Make sure that you have your logo artwork in an .eps (Encapsulated

Postscript) or .ai (Adobe Illustrator) format available to forward to your promotional product vendor. This will avoid delays caused by having to do a redrawing of your logo which could take up to several days. If you won't be able to have a clean logo ready for a rush order, be prepared to go with a simple text imprint. (See chapter on *What is Good Artwork for Imprinting?* for details.)

3. Have "Plan B" Choices. Even if you've developed relationships with your go-to suppliers and are pretty confident in their ability to have inventory available on a moment's notice, realize that there may be the occasion where stock may be low or out. Plan on making at least one or two additional "Plan B" product choices in case your "Plan A" choice fails.

4. Have Your Payment Scenario Planned. Many promotional consultants will ask for prepayment on rush orders, usually via credit card. So arrange in advance for a business credit card you will use for rush situations so you don't end up having to use your personal credit lines. Also realize that you may need to pay for expedited shipping (sometimes in advance) to meet your in-hand date.

I know I'm not alone in this gotta-get-it-now scenario. In the past few years, we have processed more rush orders than at any time in our company's history.

CHAPTER 9:
WHAT IS "GOOD ARTWORK" FOR IMPRINTING?

I can send you a .JPG file.

Can you just grab my logo off my website?

As a promotional products consultant, those are two things I never, EVER want to hear when accepting an order. Why? Because it's just about impossible for me to imprint it for you. Let's see why that is.

Usually for it to be "good artwork" for imprinting on fabric, what's required is "vector" artwork. Vector artwork is created through "mathematically defined" objects, like plotting points and drawing lines between them. The result is clean, crisp graphics are scalable, meaning that it will look essentially the same whether you use it at 1 inch or 100 inches. The graphic below on the left is a representation of a vector graphic (some resolution may be lost if you are viewing it on a screen instead of a physical book).

T Shirt Printing and Promotional Clothing Buyers Guide

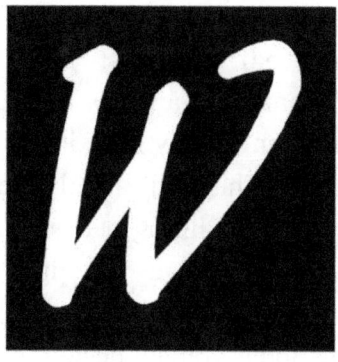 

On the other hand, "raster" artwork is a bitmap image. Bitmap images are composed of a checkerboard type grid of squares and are usually used for photographic type images. Most web type images are 72 pixels per inch (very low resolution) and those used for high resolution printing can be as high as 300 or 600 per inch. If you zoom in on a web image, you can see the squares.

The reason the clean lines are needed is because ink imprinting your logo art is usually done with a screen printing process. Think of it as somewhat like a stencil. Now imagine you have to cut the stenciled design using the rough edge graphic shown on the right. Might be less than smooth edges for sure!

Your logo designer should be able to provide you with an Encapsulated Postscript (.eps), Adobe Illustrator (.ai), or a print production quality PDF file that you can pass along to your promotional products consultant. Once you have that, your consultant can easily resize it to whatever imprint size you'll need for your project. Word of caution: Do not try to "convert" a .jpg or .gif file to an .eps or .pdf format, thinking that it will magically turn into production ready artwork. It will not. It just converts the low resolution file into a file that can be read (not used) as an .eps or print ready .pdf.

If, for some reason, you cannot get a vector art file for your project, your consultant can usually have it redrawn for you by a graphic artist. This will involve extra expense and time. So investing in hiring a designer to create imprint-ready artwork will save you time and dollars over the years.

And while we're talking about graphic design, please do yourself, your promotional product consultant, and your marketing image a favor by investing in an official logo for your business. This is the face you show to the world!

CHAPTER 10:
6 GUIDELINES GRAPHIC DESIGNERS NEED TO KNOW WHEN DESIGNING FOR T SHIRTS

Always get a kick out of looking through graphic design publications, especially when they feature award competitions for self promotion. Some of the creations are true labors of love, or maybe I should just say true labors. These direct mail or self-promotion packages are handmade arts and crafts extravaganzas. Wonder what the run was on those? Hope not more than a few dozen were made up and hope they're not recommending these kinds of labor-intensive and costly ideas to their clients. But I'll bet they are.

So that you don't get caught spending big bucks on your graphic designer's unrealistic dream project, here are several guidelines designers need to be aware of, particularly as they relate to the art being created for decorating T shirts and other promotional clothing:

1. Printing on a Non-Paper Surface is Not Like Printing on Paper. That seems obvious, right? Yet it's easy to forget that a fabric or porous surface will absorb ink, causing the imprint to spread and lose detail. For processes such as debossing on leather jackets, where the design is impressed into a surface, there is a limit to how small text and fine lines can be accommodated. Usually, your promotional products consultant can provide detailed specs or templates.

2. *Vector Art Required.* Graphic designers are well aware of the value of scalable, clean edge art in vector format. Yet I have encountered several occasions when they submit artwork with gradients and raster art for a promotional product. These are unimprintable except in some digital printing processes. Clean black and white (no gray!) artwork for ink imprints is a requirement.

3. *What Looks Great When Big, May Look Terrible When Shrunk... and Vice Versa.* Scale up a small logo for a big imprint and it may lose its appeal. Scale down a logo and you might need to change some line weights and other elements to imprint correctly. Options should be discussed with the client to avoid their disappointment.

4. *Limit Number of Colors to Limit Cost.* This should be a no-brainer for designers. However, I have had occasions where a designer cannot think of a way to reinterpret a multi-color logo into black and white art, and insists on a multi-color imprint which drives up costs.

5. *Be Aware of Limited Print Color Availability.* If a specialty ink is required for an imprint due to factors such as an unusual surface, there may be limited color options available. Also be aware that not all PMS (Pantone Matching System) colors may be available either. To perfectly match either a specialty ink or a PMS color may be an expensive venture. Standard and custom color print options should be discussed.

6. Entire Product Surface May Not Be Imprintable. Being creative as they are, designers often get really creative with what and where they want to print on a promotional product. T shirts are a prime example. They'll envision an all-over imprint that starts in the front, extends to the back, then runs up to the neck. Cool... but there are limits to what is possible on imprinting equipment. Granted, there are some decorating pros who can do this sort of thing. But it might be very, very expensive. Plus, to keep the per piece cost from being astronomical, a large quantity run is usually required. Before designing, and before getting all excited about an impossible design, determine what the limits are.

CHAPTER 11:
HOW TO IMPRINT QR CODES ON T SHIRTS

QR codes, those checkerboard-like squares also known as 2D codes, are everywhere it seems. On signs, clothing, business cards, heck, even tattoos. The beauty of them is that when scanned by a smartphone, they'll make things happen such as take you to a website, return information, send messages, and more.

But there are some issues with them that you need to be aware of when using them on T shirts...

Size. Though I've tried and used QR codes quite a bit smaller, usually about 1" square is recommended as a minimum for best scanning ability. Depending on the surface of your shirt, it may need to be larger than that to be readable.

Surface. I've seen some pretty kooky uses of QR codes including knitted and on a waffle (seriously, I saw that in a presentation). But here's the catch: It must be readable by a smartphone or other reading device. For best scanning, I suggest imprinting on only smooth surface fabrics.

Stretching. Unstretched T shirt fabric is just fine for imprinting QR codes. But realize that if it is stretched when worn, it may lose scanability. Conversely, if someone tucks the shirt into their jeans, it may scrunch the imprint together and be unreadable.

What are You Looking At?!? Please do not imprint a QR code on the front of a T shirt. It is especially awkward when women wear them, resulting in a lot of scanning of, well... do I have to explain?

Color and Contrast. You can print QR codes in colors other than black. But dark colors are suggested. Do not imprint the code in white. It will mess up the reading since what was white is now black and vice versa, a completely different code. I've tried it. On a related issue, make sure there is a definite contrast between the dark and light areas. That's why imprinting on colored surfaces is problematic. There may not be enough contrast between the surface and the code to be readable. So choose white or very light surface colors and dark imprints.

Ink Imprints Recommended. Though contrast can be achieved with it, embroidery may not be scannable due to uneven surface texture. Ink imprinting on smooth surfaces, please.

Order a Physical Production Sample. Let's call this insurance. When you are investing hundreds or even thousands of dollars in T shirts, it makes sense to do a physical (not virtual!) production sample to see if the artwork will be properly scanable on the surface and in the colors you have chosen. Say it costs you $100-$200 to do that. Better than having to pitch a $1,000 to $2,000 order because it doesn't work.

Tell What Will Happen When Scanned. Why should I scan your QR code? Business owners are sometimes so excited they actually got one of these codes that they slap it on everything, but then forget to tell people why it's important to scan it. A special offer? More info? If people are confused or wary of scanning, they won't… especially if it's a QR code being worn by a person. Marketing fail!

I think people are just enchanted with the technology right now and that the novelty will wear off. Would you want to wear a UPC pricing barcode on your clothing? Probably not. Essentially that's what you're doing when you're sportin' QR codes. Wearing barcodes. Your barcode is not your brand!

CHAPTER 12:
10 THINGS YOU NEED TO KNOW WHEN ORDERING EMBROIDERED APPAREL

A polo shirt is a polo shirt. NOT! "Polo shirt" is just a term used to describe a knit shirt that goes over the head and has a collar. So it could be used to describe hundreds and hundreds of different shirts.

Though polo shirts are the most commonly embroidered promotional clothing item, there are jackets, woven shirts, hats and more for which embroidery is the optimal decorating choice.

Adding to the number of styles to choose from, you also need to think about sizes, colors, embroidery, artwork to use... whew, that's a lot of details! So let's break down what information you really need when you are ordering branded apparel for your trade show personnel or even for everyday wear.

1. Type of Garment. Do you need polos or woven dress shirts? Either are used for trade show and event staff use, although polos tend to be the more comfortable choice.

2. Fabric. How comfortable a shirt or jacket feels is largely determined by the fabric and your group's preferences. "Jersey" has a smooth surface and is used in both polos and T shirts. "Pique" has a textured surface and is usually a bit heavier than jersey. "Jacquard" has a patterned surface that's knitted in. There are also "performance" fabrics which are designed to release sweat and keep dry—good for golf outings and other warm weather events.

3. Mens, Ladies or Unisex Styles. While many women could wear a men's shirt, a ladies cut shirt has a more flattering fit. If you have a lot of women working at your show or in your office, it is suggested to order styles that have a ladies fit. Looks better for your marketing image, feels better for them.

4. Size. Usually branded wearables are sized in Small, Medium, Large, etc. which are comparable to the same size designations in retail. So do not expect a totally custom fit. If you think sizing may be an issue, order blank samples before ordering your decorated apparel. Even though the samples are non-returnable, if you have a large quantity or dollar value order, it's worth it to be sure.

5. Quantity of Each Size. Get sizes in advance, don't guess! Since I always encourage people to go greener with their promotions, this eliminates the waste of both material and dollars that comes with over-ordering when you don't know sizes. Plus, by asking your recipients what sizes they want, it puts the onus on them for selecting a size.

6. Color of Garment. Easy, sort of. Again, if it's critical to match up a shirt color with your logo or theme, might be wise to get a sample in advance to check.

7. Location of Embroidery. For polos, woven shirts and jackets, embroidering the logo on the left chest is typical. Why? Because you usually put your name tag or embroidered name on the right so that your name is clearly visible when you shake hands. (Ah, so that's why.) Additional typical embroidery locations include the lower sleeve for polos and cuffs for long sleeve woven shirts. Note that cuff embroidery is facing upside down to the wearer so the customer can read it right side up. Other locations may be available, but it depends on the particular garment in question. Be aware, though, that embroidering in multiple or difficult locations can increase your cost dramatically.

8. Color of Embroidery. Usually you can have multiple color threads in the same logo for no additional charge. From the supplier we use, you can have up to 4 or 6 (sometimes more) colors at no additional charge; your particular supplier's maximum color limit may vary. If you have a particular PMS (Pantone Matching System) color that needs to be matched, it can be done, but it may involve additional fees.

9. Size of Embroidery. For polos, woven shirts, and jackets, around a 3" x 3" embroidered left chest logo area is typically a maximum. For polo lower sleeve and woven shirt cuffs, usually 1" x 2" is maximum (sometimes smaller). Other embroidery location sizes vary. However, always check before creating any design for embroidery.

10. Artwork. Though embroidery can emulate shading, remember that each shade in your artwork is a different thread. With shading in your logo, you'll hit that 10 color thread color maximum in a hurry. Your logo artwork must be crisp, clean, non-gradient vector artwork to achieve the best embroidery possible. See a full discussion on artwork in the chapter *What is Good Artwork for Imprinting?* which applies to both imprinted and embroidered apparel.

CHAPTER 13:
STITCH COUNT FOR CUSTOM EMBROIDERY EXPLAINED

I just want my logo embroidered on this jacket. How much will it be? My answer to that is, *It depends.* Usually I hear a disheartened sigh on the other end of the line. Unlike ink imprinting, embroidery costs can be all over the map and it all depends on the stitch count and complexity of your design. In some cases, the embroidery decoration can cost more than the actual garment itself!

What is stitch count? It is the number stitches that an embroidery machine has to make to apply your logo design to a garment. I have found that most simple design logos fall within the 5,000 to 7,000 total stitch range for application on the left chest (typical location) on an embroidered shirt or jacket, about the same for hats. Your stitch count and cost could be higher or lower, depending on these factors:

Size. Bigger Logos = More Stitches = Greater Cost. That's logical for most people to grasp.

Density. It's not just the size of your logo, it's the amount of stitches it takes to render the design. For example, let's say that the area your logo artwork covers is 3 inches by 3 inches, or 9 square inches. If your design is a lot of thin lines and some text over that area, it will be minimal coverage and less stitches. But if every square inch of that 9 square inches is covered with stitches, it will be very expensive because it takes more thread and more machine time.

Complexity. If you've got a tricky, intricate design, a decorator may assess additional handling fees.

Number of Colors. Check with your promotional products consultant for limit of thread colors you can use for your design. The size of the embroidery machine being used dictates that number. Typically, machines for logo apparel can have 1 to 6 or more embroidering heads. Again, it varies widely depending on the machine being used. In general, I recommend keeping the number of colors to 4 or 6 maximum. You may need to have your graphic designer adjust your logo to accommodate the limited colors. And make sure there is NO SHADING or GRADIENTS in the final design. Each shade or level of gradient adds 1 color thread to your design.

Digitizing. Even before your corporate apparel order gets started, your logo design must be digitized and fed into the embroidery machine. This is where the actual stitch count is calculated. Clean, vector artwork is required for best results. See the chapter on *What is Good Artwork for Imprinting?* for details.

MONEY & TIME SAVING TIP: Use the same promotional products consultant and decorating company for all your promotional apparel and digitize your logo for a size that will work in a variety of applications. That way you save on digitizing fees for future projects

T Shirt Printing and Promotional Clothing Buyers Guide

(although an edit fee may be needed for some applications) and your logo is always ready to go. Maximum size of 3" x 3" is usually good for the left chest on embroidered polo shirts and jackets, as well as accessories such as hats, golf towels and bags. Check with your consultant for suggested artwork size.

CHAPTER 14:
DEBOSSED LEATHER IMPRINTING EXPLAINED

While embroidery can be used for leather and leather-like goods, an easier, durable and sometimes less expensive imprint method is "debossing" which impresses your logo into the surface of the product, creating a subtle and sophisticated tone-on-tone look. The easiest way to explain it is that it's like a cattle brand that doesn't burn the surface.

Generally debossing is available on thicker surfaces that would respond to heat and pressure. Leather or leather-like jackets, writing portfolios, bags and wallets would be prime examples.

One caution that you must consider when preparing your logo artwork for debossing is that fine detail does not work well. In fact, details could be obliterated completely during the process. So simplifying your logo or imprint is highly recommended. Again, as with all other imprint methods discussed, good artwork is the key to getting the best impression with debossing. See the chapter on *What is Good Artwork for Imprinting?* for details.

T Shirt Printing and Promotional Clothing Buyers Guide

To see examples of debossed leather promotional products, check out this short video on our PromoWithPurposeTV YouTube channel:

http://youtu.be/3T59J3wMyhM

CHAPTER 15:
HOW TO AVOID A PUBLIC RELATIONS NIGHTMARE WHEN BUYING PROMOTIONAL CLOTHING

Let's say you're launching a fundraising campaign for a children's welfare organization. You've decided to distribute an imprinted T shirt as a thank you gift for donations. Great idea that could help spread the word about your work as the shirts are worn in the community. So you find an attractively priced T shirt online. Prices like that will help you save funds for your cause. But wait! That inexpensive price may turn into an expensive public relations nightmare. Here's how...

You might be thinking that because it is cheaper, the problem may be that it is poorly constructed or uses lower grade materials. Yes, that might be possible. But more importantly, the shirt's material or construction could have been produced in an environment or in a country that allows child, forced or prison labor. These are serious fair trade issues that are beginning to take center stage in the world marketplace.

Imagine the backlash in the press, on Twitter, and in blogs that would result by you, a supporter of a children's welfare effort, using a promotional product suspected to be made by child labor. Ouch! Your campaign will quickly go from fundraising to defense which will eat up much needed funds for your mission.

In a similar scenario, organizations that support green efforts would be well advised to look at how green their imprinted giveaways are.

Groups that support American workers should also be careful. Many flag-waving promotional items are made outside the United States' borders. You get the picture.

Whatever item you choose to market your organization must be made with materials and labor that mirror your values. Even if you are not with the organization itself, but are just a sponsor, you will be doing yourself and the group you support a big favor by selecting giveaways that are aligned with the cause.

What can help you avoid this public relations nightmare?

Clarify Your Mission, Message, and Values. Be very specific about what you are trying to accomplish and what is important to your organization.

Determine What is Unacceptable. Knowing the message you are trying to communicate, determine what aspects of a product would be contrary to that. Supporting children's welfare? No child labor. Starting an eco friendly campaign? No petroleum-based plastic products.

If in Doubt, Ask. If you cannot readily determine the fair trade or eco friendly status of a promotional product, ask your consultant. If he cannot provide you with adequate documentation or certification (such as for fair trade or organic status), it would be recommended to continue looking. Similarly, he should be able to provide the country of origin for the item in question.

CHAPTER 16:
WHAT DOES MADE IN THE USA REALLY MEAN?

"Made in the USA" sounds like a simple claim, right? But it's a little more tricky that you might think. According to the Federal Trade Commission, "Made in USA" means that "all or virtually all" the product has been made in America. Again, doesn't that sound simple?

Let's look at the example of a promotional pen. What is it made of? Plastics, some metal, ink. Let's say the plastic parts are made and metal is formed in United States' factories. The ink is brewed up here, too. But both the plastics and the inks could be composed of petroleum that was drilled from overseas. So it is still made in the USA?

This is always tricky, especially for promotional retailers like our company. We're totally dependent on our supply chains to provide us with accurate sourcing info to pass on to our customers. Not only that, in some cases, particularly for goods such as T shirts, the country of origin could change with each batch.

Most retailers, particularly in the promotional products arena, rarely identify country of origin. Don't guess! Seek out sources that make it clear if it's important to your group. From our research of a major promotional industry database, we found only about 10% of available products are sourced domestically in the United States. So if in doubt about where something was made, ask!

CHAPTER 17:
WHAT IS A UNION BUG?

Some of our clients are in or serve the union trades. Finding promotions that filled their needs for USA made products, as well as union made, proved to be quite a challenge. Many online promo shopping sites don't identify country of origin, much less whether it's union made. Then there are those that sell promotional products from overseas—where fair trade may not be standard like it is in the United States—and then imprint in a union shop so they can plop a union bug on it. We've even heard stories of companies that cut labels out of clothing to cover up overseas origins. We'll call shenanigans on all of that!

So let's talk about the union bugs and what they mean for organizations or audiences that are sensitive to Made in the USA and union issues.

First of all, a union "bug" is a small seal that is imprinted, impressed or tagged on a product to identify that it has been manufactured or produced in a union shop. This is especially critical for union affiliated or supporting organizations to imprint to show support for either their own members or members of fellow unions.

The bug typically identifies the union and the local group that manufactured and/or imprinted the item.

There are two situations where a union bug is allowed: 1) When the entire promotional product manufacture and imprinting is done by union facilities; or, 2) When ONLY the imprinting is done in a union shop. For our company, we do not offer a union bug to be placed on any item that is made outside of the United States.

Ironically, I've seen some union locals who completely disregard the union bug issue when it comes to promotional products... although they may be very vocal about supporting their rank and file membership otherwise. This is a public relations disaster waiting to happen. Be authentic, especially with promotions celebrating Labor Day. At the minimum, use Made in the USA promotional products for any effort supporting American workers.

CHAPTER 18:
IS YOUR PROMOTIONAL T SHIRT MADE OF UNNATURAL COTTON?

So I go to a "green" event and they hand out cotton canvas bags. The bags are reusable, sturdy and made from a non-petroleum product and that's good. However, conventionally grown cotton is one of the most non-eco friendly materials available for promotional T shirts and bags.

Traditionally grown cotton uses a significant percentage of insecticides and pesticides used in the entire world! Chemical fungicides, herbicides, and defoliants are also used. Even to begin with, the cotton seeds are frequently GMOs (genetically modified organisms). Natural? Hardly.

Why is this? If cotton crops are not rotated, which can be the case in traditional cotton farming, soil becomes sterile and devoid of nutrients to foster healthy crops and fend off pests and diseases. Thus the need for genetically engineered seeds which are stronger, coupled with a healthy (??) dose of chemical support. Intensive irrigation is also required. And all of this doesn't even take into consideration the land use devoted to traditional cotton farming.

Contrast conventional cotton farming with a truly natural alternative: organic cotton. Organic cotton farming starts out with untreated non-GMO cotton seeds. The seeds are planted in fields where cotton crops are rotated to increase organic matter, build fertile soil, and increase water retention capability, thus reducing water needs. Natural pest predators, trap crops, and cultivation methods are used to eliminate pesticide use. Hand weeding methods as opposed to chemicals. Those of you who are gardeners know this is quite a job!

All equipment and processing of organic cotton must be done separately from traditional cotton to avoid contamination. Organic cotton must also be certified (look for it on product information or labeling) to ensure that each bale of cotton has been grown using organic methods and that it has remained uncontaminated throughout its journey from field to factory to buyer. With all the meticulous farming, processing, and monitoring required for organic cotton, it is often more expensive than conventional cotton.

While the manufacture of organic cotton is more earth and people friendly than traditional cotton, the fact remains that land use needed to produce cotton is significant. And though land use may still be an issue, we are also seeing entries in the promotional wearable and bag market that are made from soy, bamboo, corn, and other non-cotton plant-based sources.

Would you believe it if I told you that in some cases polyester fabrics are a more eco friendly choice? Granted, polyester is not typically degradable, though it can be recyclable. And most people prefer the comfort of cotton. But here's something to consider. The acreage required to build a synthetic fabric manufacturing plant is just a fraction of the millions of acres devoted to growing cotton and the resources it takes to sustain them.

My prediction? I think we might see manmade fabric T shirts with enhanced degradability. Recycled polyester fibers are also creeping into the promotional product marketplace and help close the green loop by remanufacturing and repurposing fibers for new uses to keep them out of landfills. And alternative non-cotton, sustainable and natural fiber fabrics will continue to make inroads.

The pros, cons and costs of cotton versus polyester-based fabrics could go on for days. So what it really comes down to is what choice of fabric will be most comfortable—both physically and emotionally—with the people who will be receiving and wearing your promotional apparel.

CHAPTER 19:
HOW TO GREEN UP PROMOTIONAL T SHIRT BUYING WITH LIFE CYCLE ASSESSMENT

Have you ever thought about what happens to your imprinted T shirt after your event? It's a good question and one that you really need to think about BEFORE buying.

Ideally, of course, you'd like to think that your T shirt will be worn by recipients as they work out, shop at the store, or go to other events. Unfortunately, that's not often the case.

Here are some of the more popular post-event lives for imprinted T shirts:

Pajamas. Yes, they will have lots of market exposure while people sleep.

Car Wash Rags. Especially if they're white and don't have a lot of printing on them.

Gardening/Housework Attire. It's not appropriate enough to wear out on the street. So it's okay to mess it up while doing dirty work.

Charity/Resale Donation. Your T shirt could be going straight to the donation bin after your event.

Let's take a moment to talk about charity donations. It surprises many people to learn that charities don't always sell these castoffs in their resale stores or sent to the needy in other countries. Items that are not considered suitable for sale on a resale level are often sold by weight to jobbers who sell them to a variety of markets both here and abroad.

Also don't be disheartened by the fate of your event T shirt going somewhere other than to a needy person in another country or being shredded for other use. In the promotional arena, there is a new market for recycled fiber fabrics. Both cottons and synthetic fibers are being repurposed into new T shirts and fleece items.

Knowing the life cycle (and afterlife) of that promotional T shirt project you're planning is key to making a greener purchase. Specifically, you need to assess:

Potential Lifetime. How long, in terms of months or years, would you expect recipients to wear it? Will they wear it at the event and send it directly to the charity bin? Some of this can be determined by the quality of the shirt you choose. Higher quality or very comfortable ones, regardless of imprint, can become favorites. I've received some at athletic events that I immediately sent to the donation pile. The fabrics were cheap, itchy, wrinkly, had an imprint that used so much ink I thought I was wearing a plastic bag, or, in the case of a "tech" fabric, so hot I sweat in them instantly. Goodbye! Also, to help extend the shirt's life post-donation, opt for limiting imprint areas to expand the useful fabric area. Imprinted areas are often unusable except for possibly scrap fiber.

Your Recipients. Are your recipients T shirt wearers? I've done a lot of running events and I've observed that a lot of the runners are very unlikely to wear the event shirt at the race. Very competitive runners or athletes do NOT typically wear them on race day. They wear their training gear or, what I call, "good luck wear." They may wear the event shirt after the event, but typically not for training. Really the only ones they want are those for high profile competitive running events such as marathons. It becomes a badge of honor they'll be proud to wear after the event! But for fun runs and community type events, maybe not so much (a box of free energy bars might be more appreciated). By contrast, at a fun run/walk, you may have a lot of families where a wearable freebie might help stretch the clothing budget for kids. Plus, kids might want to show off that they were cool enough to participate. So, yes, they want them.

Collectible Potential. How much do you think you could get on eBay for a vintage 1970s rock concert T shirt? Probably a good buck! Is the promotional shirt you're buying going to promote a once-in-a-lifetime experience? Does it commemorate an up-and-coming artist that could make it valuable in the future? This may be difficult to assess. Generally, though, the higher profile the event, performer, or place visited, the more collectible market value the shirt may have down the road.

Extended Promotional Value. Shirts which promote a continuing effort, such as awareness campaigns, may have an extended life after an initial event. In this case you would be well advised to select a wear-worthy choice that is comfortable and better quality to foster continued post-event wear.

Supply Chain. Sometimes this is tricky. Most promotional online vendors rarely, if ever, identify the country of origin for T shirts. It can vary widely from product to product. As well, in the case of overseas production, source country could change rapidly should the manufacturer move operations to circumvent quota issues. I have seen T shirt samples of the exact same shirt style that have different countries of origin on each. If fair trade issues are a concern, stick with USA made T shirts. Should you be more concerned about a greener fabric content—for example, you don't want cotton made with pesticides or herbicides—then stick with organics. To be labeled organic, it must be processed separately.

Whew! That was quite a journey. Bottom line? You need to think outside the event when purchasing.

CHAPTER 20:
HOW TO START AN ECO FRIENDLY CASUAL FRIDAY

By now, Casual Fridays are a standard business practice in many companies. But what if you could take that concept one step further and encourage eco friendly values by creating Eco Friendly Casual Fridays?

An Eco Friendly Casual Friday would still allow the business casual dress code of a standard Casual Friday. However, employees would be encouraged to wear at least one piece of eco friendly apparel. Eco friendly apparel options would include items that are made with organic, sustainable, biodegradable or recycled materials. You might also want to add social consciousness categories to this list such as fair trade, USA made and union made.

Sounds easy enough. But once you start looking for the eco friendly (or fair trade) label in many popular clothing retailers, you'll find that items qualifying for one or more of these categories are scarce. What's more is that it is often impossible to determine if an item qualifies while shopping in the store. You would have to do some significant supply chain research to determine many items' qualifications.

With the retail arena scenario as it presently is, you might want to provide a way for employees to share why the item they chose to wear is eco friendly and where they purchased the item. That way they can assist fellow employees in finding good eco friendly sources and make it an educational exercise as well.

What would employees gain from this exercise? First, employees would become aware of how non-eco friendly many of their everyday purchases are. The goal would be to encourage them to vote with their wallets by redirecting spending to those items and retailers that are aligned with these values.

There may be some resistance by employees to participate because they may not share eco friendly values. So whatever you do, do not turn this into a battleground. Just make it a fun program to participate in. You might even want to start a contest to reward those who wear either the greatest number of eco friendly clothing items on a given day or those who wear the most eco friendly categories (i.e. 100% organic, post-consumer recycled, etc.). A gift card to an eco friendly clothing retailer would be an appropriate prize.

To jumpstart the program, why not consider imprinting some eco friendly promotional T shirts with your company name to distribute to your staff? That way those who may not be very interested in expending effort or money to find their own eco friendly clothing can at least participate by wearing the company-provided T shirt.

If your business is already in the eco friendly arena or instituting green initiatives, establishing an Eco Friendly Casual Friday would be a way to help bolster these values in your company and, through your employees, to the community at large.

CHAPTER 21:
SHOULD YOU SELL YOUR BRANDED T SHIRTS?

What if you could get paid for marketing your organization by selling your branded T shirts and other gear? You would offset some of the cost of your marketing and maybe create a profit center, too. Sweet!

While everyone would like to duplicate the brand extension success of an organization such as Harley-Davidson, creating a branded merchandise "store" is not for everyone. Here are scenarios where this strategy would work best:

Dedicated Customer Base United by Consumption of the Company's Main Products or Services. Biker groups, sci-fi fans, sports teams, and schools are examples. The more rabid the fan or customer base is, the more likely this strategy would be a winner.

Events. Branded promotional merchandise sold in conjunction with a special event has commemorative value. Think about the Olympics and Super Bowl.

Dealer Networks. If your customers are dealers of your products or services, they are often looking for additional ways to promote them to their customers. As well, offering authorized promotional merchandise helps you control the company image throughout the dealer network.

If your business falls into one of these categories, here are some additional considerations before you get started:

Don't Buy Huge Inventories. Until you have a sales track record, do not buy large inventories even if the per piece price is attractive. Even at a low price, unsold items waste marketing funds.

Select a Few Products to Start. Your initial store should only include a few key products to see if you get any response. Usually items such as T shirts, hats, mugs and tote bags are good initial choices.

Establish a Retail Sales Tax Number. If retail sales tax is collected by your state, you will need to establish a tax identification number if you do not have one already. You will also need to start reporting these revenues and forwarding the collected taxes to your state taxing authority. This is quite a shock to many service providers who typically do not have a retail side of their business. This will add more administrative duties to your company. So carefully consider whether the anticipated revenues are worth the additional administrative costs. Ask your bookkeeping and accounting professionals for assistance.

Designate Someone to Handle Store Activity. If handling retail type sales is not customary for your company, make sure you designate someone to monitor sales activity and order follow-up. This is a function that could easily fall through the cracks. Establishing procedures for handling is an absolute necessity.

Price it Right. Here is where you can easily make a mistake using this strategy. As with any business, you will need to add on an appropriate mark-up so that this venture does not turn into a money loser. Some companies say that because those who buy and use the branded merchandise are advertising for them, they are willing to incur a loss. There is some validity to that. But, as mentioned above, this strategy will require additional administrative effort which is not free to you.

CHAPTER 22:
THINKING BEYOND THE T SHIRT

Now that you have a better understanding of the what, why and how of purchasing T shirt printing and promotional clothing, I hope you'll be able to take what you've learned here and apply it to other promotional purchases in your future. Many of the planning and preparation steps apply whether you're buying polos, pens, paper goods or whatever serves your marketing purpose.

Wishing you the best of success!
Heidi Thorne

ABOUT HEIDI THORNE

Dr. Heidi Thorne, MBA/DBA, is an author and business speaker who focuses on small business and marketing topics. She has over 25 years of experience in sales, advertising, marketing and public relations, including a decade in the hospitality and trade show industries. As well, she was a trade newspaper editor for over 15 years, has blogged since 2010 and taught at the college level for five years.

Books. Heidi has written several books and eBooks on business and self publishing. For a current listing of all books, with links to purchase, visit the "Books" page at HeidiThorne.com.

Speaking. Need a speaker for your business event? Let Heidi engage and entertain your audience! For video previews and current topics, visit the "Speaking" page at HeidiThorne.com.

www.ingramcontent.com/pod-product-compliance
Lightning Source LLC
Chambersburg PA
CBHW061517180526
45171CB00001B/219